How to Outsmart Anyone

Smart Tactics for Gaining an Unfair Advantage in Any Situation

Robert willstone

Copyrights© Robert willstone

All rights reserved. No part of this book may be used or reproduced in any form whatsoever without written permission form the author or her publishers except in the case of brief quotations in critical articles or reviews.

THIS PAGE IS INTENTIONALLY LEFT BLANK

TABLE OF CONTENTS

INTRODUCTION

CHAPTER ONE

   The Power of Perception: How to See What Others Miss

CHAPTER TWO

   Mind Games: Mastering Psychological Tactics to Get Ahead

CHAPTER THREE

   The Art of Persuasion: Influencing Others Without Them Knowing

CHAPTER FOUR

   Strategic Listening: How to Use Information to Your Advantage

CHAPTER FIVE

   The Unpredictable Edge: How to Keep Others Guessing

CHAPTER SIX

   Negotiation Ninja: Winning Deals with Clever Techniques

CHAPTER SEVEN

   Body Language Secrets: Reading and Controlling Nonverbal Cues

CHAPTER EIGHT

   The Timing Trick: How to Use Timing to Outsmart Your Opponents

CHAPTER NINE

Deception and Disclosure: The Fine Line Between Truth and Tactics

CHAPTER TEN

The Mental Edge: Building Resilience and Staying Ahead

INTRODUCTION

How to Outsmart Anyone

In a world brimming with challenges and opportunities, the ability to outmaneuver others is a crucial skill that can set you apart. Whether you're striving to succeed in your career, excel in negotiations, or navigate complex social dynamics, knowing how to outsmart others gives you a distinct edge.

Outsmarting others isn't about deception or trickery; it's about thinking strategically, understanding human behavior, and using that knowledge to your advantage. It's about seeing the bigger picture, predicting outcomes, and making calculated moves that position you for success.

How to Outsmart Anyone: Smart Tactics for Gaining an Unfair Advantage in Any Situation is your guide to mastering these skills. This book will arm you with a range of techniques to help you gain the upper hand, whether in the boardroom, at the negotiating table, or in everyday interactions. You'll learn to anticipate others' actions, leverage key information, and apply psychological principles to influence situations in your favor.

Throughout this book, you'll explore the significance of emotional intelligence, the art of persuasion, and the subtle power of nonverbal communication. You'll develop the ability to read people, identify their vulnerabilities, and turn these insights into effective strategies. Moreover, you'll discover how to remain calm under pressure, stay a step ahead of the competition, and make decisions that consistently lead to favorable outcomes.

The ability to outsmart others isn't about being the smartest person in the room; it's about being the most perceptive and strategic. This book will teach you how to play the game with intelligence, foresight, and an acute awareness of the psychological undercurrents that influence human interactions. Whether you're aiming to advance in your career, secure better deals, or simply gain an advantage in your personal life, the strategies in this book will empower you to outthink and outmaneuver anyone you encounter.

Prepare to dive into a transformative journey that will change how you approach challenges, seize opportunities, and engage with others. By the end of this book, you'll be equipped with the knowledge and tools to consistently outsmart anyone, in any situation.

CHAPTER ONE

The Power of Perception: How to See What Others Miss

Perception is not only a passive experience in the complex dance of human relationships, but also an active, dynamic tool that has the power to dramatically affect results. Gaining insights into people and events that others might miss is possible when you know how to use perception. This chapter explores how to become more perceptive so that you may outwit opponents and obtain a tactical edge.

Comprehending Perception

The process of deciphering sensory data to create a consistent mental image of the outside world is called perception. It takes more than just looking to comprehend and interpret what you see. Combining observation, analysis, and focus enables you to discern hidden meanings and subtle indications that might yield important discoveries.

The Role of Attention

Perception begins with attention. You can improve your perception of pertinent details by concentrating your attention on particular features of a circumstance. Two primary categories of attention exist:

Selective attention is the ability to pay attention to one stimulus while disregarding others. For instance, selective attention enables you to tune out surrounding noise and focus on the words of the main speaker during a hectic conference.

Divided attention is the capacity to comprehend information from several sources at once. For example, in a negotiation, you may pay attention to nonverbal signs and simultaneously read the other party's body language to fully comprehend their position.

Skills of Observation

Being attentive is more than just seeing; it also entails taking note of and analyzing information that could otherwise go unnoticed gaining acute observing abilities entails:

Develop Your Eyes: Seek to notice details in ordinary circumstances. To improve your awareness of nonverbal clues, observe how others around you behave and express themselves in different contexts.

Contextual Awareness: It's important to comprehend the context in which observations are made. It is usually advisable to take situational aspects into consideration while analyzing an individual's behavior, as it may vary based on their surroundings.

The Ability to Intuitively

Perception is heavily influenced by intuition, which is the capacity to comprehend something without the need of conscious thought. It frequently stems from the subconscious processing of prior information and experiences. To improve your sense of intuition:

Think Back to Previous Experiences: Examine circumstances in which you were successfully led by your intuition. Recognizing these occurrences can you in building and improving your intuitive skills.

Be Open-Minded: Steer clear of dogmatic thought habits. Having an open mind to different options enables your intuition to provide you more precise insights.

Biases in Perception

Recognize the biases in your perception that can be caused by your perception. Typical biases consist of:

Confirmation bias is the tendency to ignore contradicting data in favor of information that supports your preconceived notions.

The "halo effect" obscures judgment by making you believe that someone who excels in one area must also excel in others.

In order to combat these prejudices, make an effort to find different viewpoints and question your presumptions.

Realistic Methods for Improving Perception

Mindfulness Practices: To improve your awareness and focus, practice mindfulness. You can learn to be more aware of the details of your surroundings and the current moment by practicing techniques like meditation.

Engage in active listening by giving the speaker your whole attention, comprehending what they're saying, and offering comments. This enhances your awareness of subtle verbal and nonverbal clues.

Develop empathy by placing yourself in other people's situations. Gaining insight into their viewpoints and feelings can improve your ability to perceive things clearly and make better decisions.

Utilizing Perceptual Ability

Integrating perceptual skills into a variety of settings is necessary for their effective application:

In negotiations, use your sense of perception to determine the other party's requirements and reactions, then modify your approach accordingly.

Resolution of Conflicts: Pay attention to the feelings and underlying problems in disputes. Understanding the underlying causes can help you address the actual issues and come up with workable solutions.

Leadership: You can lead more successfully if you have perceptual skills. These talents assist you comprehend the dynamics, strengths, and limitations of your team.

CHAPTER TWO

Mind Games: Mastering Psychological Tactics to Get Ahead

Subtle yet effective psychological strategies can be used to your benefit in a variety of situations. If you can efficiently navigate complex social landscapes and shape perceptions, you can also influence others. This chapter examines the fundamental psychological strategies that can offer you an advantage and explains how to use them tactically.

Comprehending Psychological Strategies
Psychological strategies use psychological concepts to affect decisions and behavior. They rely on your ability to perceive other people's thoughts, emotions, and behaviors in order to influence interactions in your advantage.

Important Psychological Ideas
Reciprocity: This principle is predicated on the notion that people feel compelled to repay concessions or benefits. You may instill a sense of obligation in others by providing something of

value, which increases their likelihood of complying with your requests.

Consistency and Commitment: People want to come across as consistent in the things they commit to. You can make it more likely that someone will agree to bigger requests down the road by getting them to commit to a smaller one first.

Social Proof: Individuals frequently observe other people to get behavioral indications. You can persuade others to adopt a specific behavior by showcasing instances of other people doing it.

Scarcity: Something's perceived value may rise when there is a sense of restricted availability. You can increase the appeal of your offers by instilling a sense of exclusivity or urgency.

Methods for Using Psychological Strategies
The method known as "foot in the door" Begin with a modest, amenable request. Once they consent, progressively ask for more. This approach makes use of the concepts of dedication and regularity.

Using the Door-in-the-Face Method: Make a big, irrational request first, which is probably going to be denied, and then a smaller, more logical one after that. In contrast, the lesser request appears more reasonable, which raises the possibility of compliance.

The Low-Ball Technique: Make an alluring offer or proposition, then once an agreement is reached, disclose further expenses or requirements. It is difficult for the person to withdraw from the initial offer because of the commitment made.

Developing Reciprocity: To instill a sense of duty, make modest gestures of kindness like compliments or help. To prevent coming out as manipulative, be sure that everything you do is sincere.

Negotiations Using Psychological Tactics in Action: Make the first concessions in order to persuade the other party to reciprocate, then apply reciprocity. Utilize social evidence by citing examples of how other have agreed to similar terms.

Sales and Marketing: Draw attention to one-time specials or limited-edition offerings to capitalize on scarcity. Make use of social proof by displaying client endorsements and comments.

In order to resolve conflicts, reach tiny points of agreement between the parties before tackling more important ones. This requires consistency and commitment. Reciprocity should be used by addressing their worries and making concessions.

Moral Aspects to Take into Account
Although psychological strategies might be useful, they must be applied morally. Steer clear of dishonesty and manipulation. Make an effort to influence in a way that is kind and advantageous to all parties.

CHAPTER THREE

The Art of Persuasion: Influencing Others Without Them Knowing

You may quietly and successfully influence the thoughts, feelings, and behaviors of people by using the strong ability of persuasion. Learning how to persuade others requires an understanding of human psychology as well as the use of strategies that achieve desired results without resorting to forceful means.

The Foundations of Convincing
Persuasion is the art of subtly influencing someone to reach a desired opinion or take an action. Making the decision to agree or act look like the person's own choice is all about presenting your case in a way that fits with their values and interests.

Essential Persuasion Strategies
Developing Rapport: People are more open to your influence when you connect with them and earn their trust. To establish rapport, use mirroring strategies, attentive listening, and sympathetic answers.

Framing: Emphasize the positive aspects of the content while downplaying any possible negative aspects. Your suggestion will appear more enticing and in keeping with the person's objectives if it is framed well.

Anchoring: Provide a starting point of knowledge (anchor) that shapes further assessments and choices. For instance, if you discuss a higher price first and then present a lower one, the lower price will appear to be the better offer.

Using Persuasive Language: Pay close attention to the words you use to arouse feelings and conform to the person's values. The persuasiveness of sentences that highlight advantages, common objectives, and favorable results can be increased.

Methods of Gently Persuasion
The "Yes" Ladder: Begin with modest demands that are simple to grant before moving on to more ambitious ones. Every accord intensifies the momentum and raises the possibility of obedience with subsequent requests.

The "Foot-in-the-Mouth" Technique: Make a request that is consistent with a principle or value that the other person has vocally agreed to. This instills a sense of duty and consistency.

The method known as "foot-in-the-door": Like the "Yes" ladder, just requiring a minimal commitment in order to allow for larger demands. Starting with a request that fits with the person's values or perception of themselves is crucial.

Appealing to Emotions: To inspire action, appeal to feelings of fear, enthusiasm, or empathy. Arguments based only on logic may not always be as persuasive as emotional appeals.

Persuasion in Action: In sales and marketing, emphasize a product or service's advantages by using framing. To promote trust and receptivity in client encounters, use rapport-building strategies.

Leadership: Align team goals with organizational objectives by using compelling language and framing. Establish a good rapport with your teammates to inspire and drive them to work better.

In personal relationships, use tactful persuasion to resolve disputes and reach agreements. Make emotional appeals to develop relationships and settle disputes.

Moral Persuasion
Persuasion that is ethical respects other people's autonomy and well-being. Make sure that your influence is in line with the person's best interests and refrain from using manipulative methods. Instead of misleading or coercing, the intention is to promote sincere cooperation and agreement.

CHAPTER FOUR

Strategic Listening: How to Use Information to Your Advantage

To obtain understanding, comprehend others, and use information to further your objectives, you must develop the crucial talent of strategic listening. Using the information you gather to your advantage, this chapter covers active listening techniques.

Effective Listening Is Crucial.
Extending beyond just auditory comprehension, strategic listening entails a proactive interaction and analysis of the conveyed data. Listening well enables you to discern chances for influence, as well as the speaker's point of view and ulterior motivations.

Important Skills for Listening
Pay attention to what the speaker is saying, how they are saying it, and how they are looking. Verbal affirmations and nonverbal indicators like

nodding and maintaining eye contact can both be used to demonstrate your level of engagement.

Reflective Listening: To make sure you grasp what the speaker has said, paraphrase or summarize it. This method shows that you are paying attention and invites more explanation if necessary.

Empathetic listening involves seeing oneself in the speaker's position and trying to grasp their motivations and feelings. By establishing rapport and trust, empathic listening increases the speaker's openness to your influence.

Critical listening involves analyzing and assessing the information that is being shared. Determine the main point, evaluate its veracity, and think about how it fits in with your goals.

Methods for Using Data Strategically and Recognizing Important Data: Pay close attention to important elements that highlight the speaker's needs, goals, and worries. Make use of this information to customize your offers and responses so that they meet their needs.

Leveraging Insights: Use the knowledge amassed to successfully negotiate, shape decisions, and settle disputes. For instance, tailor your proposal or sales pitch based on the needs that the client has specified.

Building Relationships: To fortify bonds and foster trust, apply the knowledge gleaned from strategic listening. Interactions might be more fruitful if you show that you appreciate and comprehend the viewpoints of others.

Preventing Obstacles: Recognize the prejudices and presumptions that could influence your listening. Refrain from making snap decisions or assumptions based on little knowledge.

Using Strategic Listening in Action: During negotiations, make use of strategic listening to ascertain the interests and position of the other party. Adapt your negotiating approach in light of the new knowledge to reach win-win agreements.

Use active listening strategies in sales and marketing to learn about the requirements and preferences of your customers. Make the most of this information by providing solutions that meet their needs and raise the possibility of a sale.

Leadership: Use thoughtful, sympathetic listening to ascertain the goals and concerns of your team. Apply this knowledge to resolve conflicts and create a productive workplace.

CHAPTER FIVE

The Unpredictable Edge: How to Keep Others Guessing

In a number of circumstances, keeping a surprising advantage can be very beneficial. You have the upper hand by throwing others off balance and making it difficult for them to predict your intentions or behaviors. The methods for fostering unpredictability and making the most of it are covered in this chapter.

The Ability to Be Unpredictable

By instilling doubt and hesitancy in others, your unpredictable nature might endear you to others. People are less likely to successfully oppose your strategies or sway your decisions when they are unable to predict your actions or reactions.

Methods of Fostering Unpredictability
Change Your Conduct: Refrain from settling into routines. Variate your reactions, routines, and

decision-making procedures to keep people guessing. Change up your negotiating strategies or communication approach, for instance.

Strategic Silence: Make the most of your pauses and quiet times. A deliberate lack of speech can make others uncomfortable and encourage them to fill the space with details or compromises.

Managed Disclosure: Disclose just pertinent details to engender a sense of mystery. If you give away too little information about your goals or strategies, people could assume the wrong thing.

Changing Tactics: Be ready to abruptly alter your approach or strategy. Being adaptive and flexible can help you stay one step ahead of others and keep them guessing about what you're going to do next.

Negotiations' Effects of Unpredictability: Make use of your unpredictable nature to gain power by leaving the other party in the dark about your priorities and ambitions. This may result in compromises and improved conditions.

Leadership: To keep your team members from being complacent, continue to make unpredictable decisions. This can help your company develop an agile and responsive culture.

Resolution of Conflicts: Employ erratic strategies to resolve disputes in fresh ways. This can upend long-held beliefs and inspire original thinking.

Finding a Consistency-Unpredictability Balance Unpredictability has its benefits, but it must be balanced with a commitment to fundamental concepts and ideals. Make sure your unpredictable behavior doesn't damage your reputation or dependability. Retaining a constant moral compass will enable you to properly handle uncertainty.

CHAPTER SIX

Negotiation Ninja: Winning Deals with Clever Techniques

Proficiency in negotiation is essential in both work and social settings. Gaining success in negotiations can be achieved by using astute negotiating strategies. Advanced negotiating techniques that can provide you an advantage and enable you to accomplish your objectives are covered in this chapter.

The Essentials of Bargaining

Achieving mutually beneficial agreements is essential to effective negotiating. Effective negotiators are aware of the fundamentals of the art and use techniques to reach win-win agreements.

Astute Bargaining Strategies

Research and Preparation: Make sure you fully understand the needs, interests, and negotiation background of the opposing side. Your ability to adjust your strategy and predict their reactions will improve with increased knowledge.

Anchoring: Make an opening offer that establishes the parameters of the negotiation. Subsequent bids and concessions may be influenced by this anchor point.

The best course of action in the event that a negotiated agreement cannot be reached is to be aware of your options. Possessing a solid BATNA gives you leverage and improves your bargaining position.

Mirroring and matching: To establish rapport and foster a sense of alignment, gently model the actions, words, and tone of the other party. Using this tactic can increase the other party's openness to your suggestions.

The "Nibble" Technique: Once an understanding has been reached, ask for a few more little compromises. The "nibble" tactic is requesting small additions that can improve the bargain overall.

Practical Negotiation Strategies for Price Negotiations: Establish an initial price using anchoring, then use your BATNA to bolster your position. Utilize the "nibble" tactic to get more concessions.

When making a business deal, find out what the priorities and interests of the opposing side are. Use cunning strategies to negotiate advantageous terms and use mirroring to establish rapport.

Conflict Resolution: Use negotiating strategies to settle disagreements and identify points of agreement. To assist in facilitating a just and efficient resolution, use anchoring and BATNA.

Moral Aspects to Take into Account
Even though you can increase your success in negotiations by using cunning strategies, it's crucial to maintain ethics. Steer clear of misleading strategies and make sure your approach promotes mutual respect and trust. Strive for solutions that are win-win for both sides.

CHAPTER SEVEN

Body Language Secrets: Reading and Controlling Nonverbal Cues

In communication, body language is extremely important and frequently conveys more information than spoken words. Comprehending and managing nonverbal cues can improve your capacity for persuasion and communication. The subtleties of body language are explored in this chapter, along with tips for making the most of them.

How Vital Body Language Is
Body language is the collection of nonverbal cues that describe intents and feelings through posture, gestures, and facial expressions. Body language has the power to improve rapport, change people's views, and improve communication.

Important Components of Body Language:
Expressions on the Face: These convey feelings and reactions. Smiles, frowns, and raised

eyebrows are important facial expressions to watch out for since they might convey emotions like delight, perplexity, or surprise.

Gestures: Nods, hand gestures, and other motions can support spoken communication by sending messages. Open motions, for instance, can convey candor and openness, whereas closed movements might imply defensiveness.

Posture: A person's standing or sitting position might convey their level of comfort, confidence, or engagement. Bending forward can convey curiosity, but crossing one's arms can convey resistance or defensiveness.

Eye Contact: Maintaining eye contact is a strong sign of sincerity and attention. While avoiding eye contact may indicate discomfort or dishonesty, maintaining adequate eye contact can strengthen trustworthiness and create intimacy.

Managing Your Own Nonverbal Cues
Conscious Awareness: Recognize the effects of your own body language on other people.

Maintaining an open and assured stance is important, as is using gestures to further emphasize your points.

Mirroring: To establish rapport and a feeling of congruence, subtly mimic the body language of the other person. The other individual may become more at ease and responsive as a result of this strategy.

Controlled Expressions: Use your face to communicate the right feelings and responses. Refrain from expressing irritation or frustration with your facial expressions since this can ruin the conversation.

Understanding Body Language in Various Negotiation Contexts: Observe nonverbal clues to determine how the other person is reacting, then modify your strategy accordingly. For instance, whilst nodding can suggest agreement, crossed arms may show resistance.

Leadership: Exude confidence and establish a good rapport with your team by using positive body language. Foster transparent communication by exemplifying engaging and transparent nonverbal actions.

Interpersonal Interactions: Read others' intents and feelings by their body language. Make the most of this knowledge to improve communication and reply properly.

Moral Aspects to Take into Account
Avoid manipulating nonverbal clues, even though mastering and interpreting body language can improve communication. Make sure your body language promotes sincere connections and complies with moral standards.

CHAPTER EIGHT

The Timing Trick: How to Use Timing to Outsmart Your Opponents

Achieving achievement and influencing outcomes need careful consideration of timing. Knowing when to take action, hold off, or adjust is essential to perfecting the timing art. This chapter delves into sophisticated tactics for taking advantage of chances and outwitting adversaries through timing.

Recognizing Timing
Selecting the ideal time to take action or make choices in order to optimize impact is known as timing. A combination of strategic planning and flexibility is needed for effective timing, which enables you to take advantage of opportunities and adjust to changing conditions.

The Fundamentals of Timing
Timing your actions strategically entails

organizing and setting up to capitalize on particular opportunities. Evaluate the surroundings and determine when it will be best to carry out your goals.

Opportunistic Timing: Take advantage of unplanned possibilities by staying vigilant and adaptable. Timing opportunistically entails spotting and seizing unanticipated opportunities that fit your objectives.

Delay: Occasionally, it can be better to wait for the ideal opportunity to act than to take instant action. Delaying your answer until better circumstances arise is known as delayed action.

Methods to Become an Expert in Timing Situational Intelligence: Gain a high sense of situational awareness to identify when to take appropriate action. To help you choose the right time, pay attention to indications, patterns, and alterations in your surroundings.

Scenario Planning: Plan ahead for several timing circumstances and possible outcomes by using scenario planning. This strategy aids in keeping you flexible and organized under changing circumstances.

time Feedback: Assess the results of your time choices in order to improve your strategy. Examine your successes and failures to make future adjustments to your timing methods more effective.

Utilizing Timing in Various Situations
Timing is a crucial tool in negotiations as it can help you gain an edge or make concessions. The negotiation process and results might be affected by the timing of your offers and replies.

Speaking in Front of an Audience: Align your main points and pauses well to keep the audience interested and highlight crucial issues. Your presentation's effect can be increased with appropriate timing.

Business Strategy: Use time management techniques to introduce new goods, break into markets, or raise capital. Timely decisions can help you stand out from the competition and provide your company an advantage.

Juggling Time and Imagination

While timing is important, keep in mind that you also need to be able to change course quickly when needed. If you become too dependent on timing and lose your ability to be adaptable and receptive to new information, you may miss out on chances.

CHAPTER NINE

Deception and Disclosure: The Fine Line Between Truth and Tactics

In strategic encounters, disclosure and deception are essential components. Being able to walk the thin line between strategy and reality can improve your capacity to influence others and accomplish goals. The ethical issues and methods for handling disclosure and deceit are covered in this chapter.

The Significance of Disclosure and Deception
While disclosure entails openly disclosing information, deception entails purposefully misleading people in order to obtain an advantage. It takes strategic planning and ethical deliberation to strike a balance between these components.

Effective Trickery Methods
Use deception to draw attention away from your genuine goals or intentions. This tactic entails

drawing attention to unrelated or false information for other people.

Selective Disclosure: In order to affect perceptions and results, only part or controlled information should be shared. With selective disclosure, you can safeguard your strategic interests while guiding others' understanding.

Fake Ignorance: To deceive adversaries or obtain a tactical advantage, behave as though you are ignorant of important information. Pretending to be ignorant can lead to unanticipated moves.

Moral Aspects to Take into Account
Openness versus Deception: Strike a balance between strategy and transparency to prevent manipulation. Make sure that using deceit doesn't compromise moral principles or trust.

Effect on Relationships: Take into account how lying could affect credibility and relationships. Use deceptive strategies sparingly and ethically because they have the potential to undermine confidence if exposed.

Legal and Moral Boundaries: When employing

deceit, respect the law's and moral standards. Make sure your strategies don't contravene any legal or moral requirements.

Disclosure Techniques

Strategic Disclosure: Determine the information's strategic value and decide when and how to share it. Strategic disclosure is the act of disclosing information to further your objectives.

Establishing Credibility: To gain others' trust and confidence, be transparent. Open communication can improve your influence and fortify bonds with others.

Managing Expectations: To prevent miscommunications or letdowns, establish reasonable expectations through transparency. Managing people' views and responses can be facilitated by open and sincere communication.

CHAPTER TEN

The Mental Edge: Building Resilience and Staying Ahead

To keep an advantage in demanding and competitive situations, mental toughness must be developed. By building resilience, you can continue moving toward your objectives, remain focused, and overcome hardship. Keeping ahead of the game and developing mental toughness are topics covered in this chapter.

Knowing What Mental Resilience Is
The capacity to overcome obstacles, get back up after failures, and keep a positive attitude is known as mental resilience. Stress management, overcoming challenges, and maintaining goal focus are all skills of resilient people.

Methods for Developing Hardiness
Developing an optimistic outlook will help you better manage obstacles. Maintaining motivation

and desire requires concentrating on solutions rather than issues.

Control Your Stress: Learn stress-reduction strategies like mindfulness, physical activity, and rest. Resistant to hardship, you might become more resilient and overall well-being.

Establish attainable goals in order to give yourself direction and meaning in life. Setting goals enables you to maintain motivation and focus in the face of adversity.

Adaptability: Develop adaptability by being flexible and prepared to modify your tactics. People that are resilient may change course and adjust to new situations while still achieving their goals.

Ways to Stay Ahead: To stay ahead of the competition, make a commitment to lifelong learning and personal growth. Learn new talents, information, and perspectives to improve your capacity and stay current with changing fashions.

Networking: To obtain opportunities, resources, and support, establish and utilize a strong network. You may stay ahead of the curve in your profession by using the insights and valuable contacts that networking can offer.

Making Self-Care a Priority

It is essential to look after your emotional and physical well-being. Increasing your resilience and sustaining high performance in all facets of life requires regular physical activity, a well-balanced diet, and adequate sleep.

Overcoming Obstacles

Learn from Setbacks: Consider setbacks as chances for personal development rather than as obstacles to overcome. Examine what went wrong, draw important conclusions, and improve your strategy.

Seek Guidance: Don't be afraid to ask professionals, peers, or mentors for help when you're having problems. They can provide new insights and motivation that are helpful in getting beyond challenges.

Remain Determined: Despite obstacles, never

lose sight of your long-term objectives. People that are resilient never waver in their quest for achievement and never stop moving forward.

www.ingramcontent.com/pod-product-compliance
Lightning Source LLC
Chambersburg PA
CBHW070949220526
45471CB00007B/2959